MW01248646

Moonlit Musings

Caitlin Salovich

Presentation by *BookLeaf Publishing*

Web: www.bookleafpub.com

E-mail: info@bookleafpub.com

ISBN: 9789358367607

First edition 2023

To the bravest of us, who choose healing above all else,
as our evolutionary process. This journey to meet
your soul self is your lifetime's greatest work.

INDEX

found in oasis

Where the wild wind races
And the trees gallop, so the river may ignite
a spectacle of unmet horizons,

That is where you'll uncover a

daydream of the beginning.

nightscape

The moon beats purple
On a periwinkle dance,

Inviting mistress stars
For a night-away dreamland.

solace

Perplexing midnight
an alone existence
grasping to face paranoia
with the fortune of destiny.

Hunting for the purpose of creations
Falling short, inevitably
an improbable coincidence.

Why must there be an explanation for all wonderful
things?

expressions

Conquering love
And everything in between.

Two souls paired
matching mirror reflections.

Lovers from finish to start
Where no ending is every beginning.

sacred empath

Capable and curious being of light,
channels of mystery run reckless
at your cosmic core.

Your eyes quake with justice.

An electric universe
carried inside your every delicate detail.

there is so much healing here

soul signed, your higher self

unsent expectations

Electric neon-colored sky,
Intoxicating clouds
of charming mood pinks.

Melancholy lips invite desires
craving for devotions

Request permission with your eyes -

An invitation to enter herein..

mid summer

Meet the white rose enchantment:
Elegant mischief, simply unraveling.

Gentle fragrances of long-lost summers ago
chasing my buttercream nose.

Floating in safe-haven daytime dreams,
Where innocence never leaves or remains.

This can be loving you.

meet your shadow

Sacred is the space for change,
Unapologetic and forgiving.

A path with no occupied footsteps
Led by courageous certainty.
Envisioning realities to where they exist

A dramatic split of the ego
Shedding past livelihoods
Overflowing lightness

Acceptance is first.

Here you are.

transient vagabond

Stars whisper touching lullabies
While the ocean covertly mourns
A silk honeymoon watches all
Like a casted outsider.

Distance is illusionary.
Experiences performing,
Connections based in free-will.

So where do you find refuge on the darkest of
nights?

inaudible echo

I often wonder who you are
before the world invented your mask

And so thoughtfully captured
your illuminating face

Who taught you how to hide everything and feel
only the most insufferable?

You deemed the world unsafe
Retreated to your inner sanctuary
Constructing a delusion
where your learned survival ways
were forever justified.

The coldness you carry and a bitter
Heart showcased for any
kindness displayed.

A stolen desire for connection
buried under stacked emotions
suffocating in shame and self-hatred.

Existing only as an illusion.
A wild card
Joker.

The disease of un-loving. It wrecks
Even the most beautiful of souls.

A narcissist's poem.

lovers not lost

I will place you on a shelf,
in the room of my heart adorned.
painted in fondness
tucked away pleasantly.

A monument of last love's lesson.

rescue letter

formally you,

exercise boundaries with
those who threaten your memories.
Convincing forced narratives and one-sided
appreciation
to serve only absurd demands.

Influencing a mind
and conceiving what never was
is a tactic perfected by those
who live to entrap you.

Observe their efforts with careful consideration.
Learn to read paranoia in pupils
and decipher lying lips.

Let not your heart be unguarded for careless
Intruders.
Thieves by discretion.

Disguised, *love bandit*.

you

A heart-driven
moonstone
escaped my idle gaze.

Descending
into portals
spanning my reality.

Phenomenal.
remarkable.
infinite.

believe in me

fuck you (fuck boy)

Forgive me,
(Fuck You)

While I say a final goodbye to our past.
(To love you was an unholy mistake)

Wreaked with havoc and frustrations,
(And I cannot afford delusions with my heart)

A "catch-me-if-you-can-" style gameplay.
(Toxic anxious/avoidant replays)

I can no longer offer my heart to you.
(I wish you healing above all else)

An honest *(fuck you)* farewell

man-ifested

And then, just like that, one day - perhaps
on a regular Thursday,
You will encounter who has been waiting to
Welcome you
Here as you are.

In every existence

Full transparency in love and intentions,
blossoming to reciprocate.

A man-infested vision of identical soul songs.

always forever, yours

fantasia

Find me again when the moon is cockeyed white,
wake me when the golden thistles splash the
Wicked grapevine.

Destined for star-gazed slumberings,
and nights never found again.

When I was with you, once.

Imagined.

he/she-motionally unavailable

Desperation washed off regretful skin.
Pulling for pieces
not yet/never for sale.

Unqualified to reveal soul coordinates.

Are we chasing an ending we
know can never exist?

Both unwilling to decide.

shadow/self

What looks intricate in the shadows
once exposed to the light,
Reveals many flaws and vulnerabilities.

Fear is a master complicator.
A seductive camouflage laid
delicately over the mind's eye.

Pure blackout voluntary.
Lingering comfortable in your
own darkness.
Complete surrendering of self.

Will you meet you as you are?

child's play

Love yourself so wildly
as to never accept stale
breadcrumbings of affection
and relentless ego-worship
as your own moments of validation

Give gracious goodbyes to temporary
pleasures and self-imposed limitations.

Dismiss those with vile intentions and
beguiling promises

Any unsacred word offering
met with a straightforward refusal

boundaries enforced
will eradicate the unhelpful.

once karmic partners

Jaded by potential, a luring hopefulness
Inconsistencies bittersweet
Rest assured my empathy comforting,
Offered sanctuary in a broken palace

Little did you know I was picking up pieces
Building a strong foundation for myself

And pulling up out of the intertwined chaos
Of another burdened soul

Your love was not my anchor
It was a warning call

Meant to derail me from another
Forsaken path
One stuck in survival alone

Armed with awareness
And no tolerance for personal peace disruption

Perhaps only a figment
Of perpetual distorted imaginations

Trauma bonding at its finest

narcotic

Absent embraces evoke
memories of your heartfelt company
once upon a life

physical sincerity has no space for dishonesty
nor bad intentions. Simplification amplified.
Intimacy impossible to imitate

An entanglement nurturing
attention, captivated by essence

To receive one's entire humanness,
a brief dance of inner light.

A divine soul connection download.

Effortlessly mine.

Printed in the USA
CPSIA information can be obtained
at www.ICGtesting.com
LVHW010547021223
765241LV00091B/3485